The Crowns I Wear

By

Deidre Silas

Preface

As women we tend to play many roles and wear many crowns in our lives. I personally have worn several in the last 10 years of my life. Some I wear with pride, and some taught me a life lesson. Nevertheless, they made me who I am today. I'm grateful to them because they gave me the strength to write this book. The purpose of this book is to merely share some of my experiences about crowns that I wore and what I went through while wearing them. My goal for this book is that readers take how important selfcare is and to reach out to someone when you're at that breaking point.

"Ambition is priceless, it's something that's in your veins. And I put that on my name."

~Wale

Table of Contents

Chapter One

Career Woman

1ˢᵗ Day

On December 21, 2009 at 5:30am I stepped foot into an all-male juvenile facility not knowing what to expect. I spent the first 15 minutes in a room called the "role call room" listening to the supervisor call everyone's name. As they call my name, they told me who I would be paired with for the day. As I stood there waiting for roll call to end, I thought to myself, "Deidre is this what you want to do for the rest of your life? The answer to my own question was "No, it's a means to an end". I left the roll call room with the two male staff I was partnered with for the day and started on a long path to what was know as "The Circle". The Circle was four housing units that figuratively speaking made a circle. I walked into the building titled "Pierce" to see two African American young men that couldn't be no more than 16- or 17-years old cleaning up the day room area. The staff that I was paired with lead me into the small control room while the other staff walked down one of the wings of the housing unit. As we are sitting in the control room the overnight staff gave us a rundown of how the night went. We then proceeded to read through what was know as the "logbook". This book was were staff communicated with each other on a regular basis. As I'm reading through the book, I could hear the other staff yelling at the top of his lungs for everyone to wake up followed my inmates hurling insults at the staff for being loud. I proceed to ask the staff I was with "why does he have to be so loud?" and the staff responded, "it's just what he does". I was then given a breakdown of what the day would entail. I was informed that our day starts out with wake up, clean up, breakfast, school, lunch and back to school in that order. As the other staff begins to let the inmates out of their rooms, they begin to file into the dayroom area. As I'm standing in the office, they all begin to stare at me through the thick glass, whispering amongst themselves. I will admit I felt a little intimated because I felt like a fish in a fishbowl being stared at in amazement. Upon stepping out of the control room one inmate approached me and asked, "what's your name?", I replied "Ms. Graham". The staff yelled for everyone to step out. The inmates then began to file out the front door one by one. Once outside the staff with the clip board began to take roll and call off each inmate's name. He then proceeded to do a head count to ensure each person was accounted for. As we began to line up with 48 inmates to the left of us, I see the staff I am with take out his radio and say, "Pierce requesting a 10-59 from Pierce Cottage to the Dietary with a count of 48 and 3". As we stood in the freezing cold, I saw a white van appear and informed us via radio that our "10-59 was clear to proceeded". As we were walking the van followed behind us slowly and I asked myself again "is this what you really want to do with your life?" and the answer still remained the same "No". As we walked into the dining room we were greeted by supervisors and dining room staff. The inmates were told to line up against the wall. As they stood in line the lady behind the counter who was supervising inmates serving the food proceeded to tell the inmates in line "two at time". The inmates followed the commands given and proceeded to go through the serving line to get their breakfast trays. After collecting their trays, they proceed to sit at the tables in room order. As they are sitting the staff began to take a head count of all the inmates again. As I look on the staff tells me "you see this tracking sheeting right here, this is what helps you keep your job, always know where your inmates are and how many you got". As the inmates are eating, I observed that there was another group of inmates to the left of us finishing up their breakfast. I then hear someone yell "Bus Down". That made me laugh a little. As our inmates were eating the staff informed them that they had 5 minutes left. As the dining room worker proceeds to bring the garbage cart to collect trays he begins to stare me up and down. This made me a little uncomfortable because as a woman its very unusual to see a young man that age look at you like a piece of meat. Once all the trays were collected the young men were told to line up "A-wing on the glass and B-wing in the middle". One of the staff then began to do pat down searches of the inmates to ensure that they didn't have any food or contraband on them. Another head count is taken as we proceed to walk out of the dining room. As we stepped outside the same white van was already waiting for us. The staff gets on the radio an says "Pierce requesting a 10-59 from the Dietary to the School, 48 and 3". The staff in the van states "you are clear to step with a count of 48 and 3". As we are walking to the school, I couldn't help but to observe the amount of old condemned buildings all over the facility grounds. As we stepped into the school the inmates were told to stand on the yellow line. The staff then proceeded to give their clip board to the staff at the front desk at the school. The staff at the desk then proceed to inform inmates whose teachers were out for the day to step to the library. We were then instructed to take the remaining inmates upstairs to the second floor. As we filed up the stairs the inmates were told no talking and to stay on the yellow line. As I watched teachers stand outside of their classrooms as we made our way around the hall inmates began to step off into various classrooms. I saw one teacher hand an inmate something. Once we made our way around the entire second floor and all the inmates were in their classes. I asked the staff I was with what did the teacher give the inmate. He stated, "caught being good ticket". The teachers apparently gave these tickets out to the inmates that were doing what they were supposed to be doing and if they collect a certain amount then they would be placed in a drawing for a donut. I said to the staff "a treat for being good, like you would a dog". He replied, "you catch on fast rookie". As the morning went on in the school various inmates began sticking their heads out the classrooms and beckoning me saying "CO I need to talk to you" and out of nowhere I responded, "my name's not CO, its Ms. Graham and no go back to class". That would begin my journey of "no" being my response to anything that was asked of me. Around 11am they announced over the intercom for Pierce cottage to dismiss. I along with the two male staff I was working with positioned ourselves in the hallway to gather the inmates for our housing unit. We proceeded to step down the stairs and collected our clip board from the front desk staff. We proceeded to take roll and then stepped out the building. The staff then informed me that he wanted me to call for an escort to the dining room for lunch. As I pulled the radio from my holster, I said to myself, "don't mess this up". As I opened my mouth the words just flowed, "Security Pierce is requesting a 10-59 from the school to the dining room with 48 and 3". Security arrived and began to trail us as we walked to the dining room. We proceeded into the dining for lunch. Once they ate, we proceeded to line up and called for a security escort and headed back to the school. We would spend the remainder of the day in the school until we were relieved by the evening shift staff. We proceeded to inform them how the day went and what the unit count was. As I made the journey back to the main gate, the staff I was working began to ask what I thought about my first day. I told him it was cool and that I would have to see how the rest of the week went. When I got to my car, I sat there for about 15 minutes before pulling off and thought to myself "are you ready, can you do this and is this really what you want to do for the rest of your life".

C.O.

As the years went on, I became extremely well at my job. I learned so much from the veteran staff that I worked with both a male and female. Little did I know they were preparing me for the life of a Correctional Officer (CO) as the inmates called us. I'm now five years into my career and I have seen it all and heard it all. Being a female correctional officer in an all-male juvenile facility is not the easiest job by far. This is not for the weak hearted. You need a tough skin but even people with tough skin can break sometimes. It's a high stress job that can sometimes come with long hours. If you're not careful you can get sucked in by the amount of money that you make. I for instance was one of those people. I began pulling double shifts at least 4 days week and was making about $60k to 65k a year. You become institutionalized and see the prison as a second home. You form bonds with your coworkers because no one outside the gate understands what you go through daily but the people that you work with. They become your second family. You pick up the prison lingo and you sometimes forget where you are, and you use it in your home life that people look at you strange because they don't know what you're talking about. I even began to curse more, and small things would set me off and make me angry. At times I thought to myself if my mother was to see me, she would say that's not my child. You become more self-aware and you're on constant guard. You must position yourself so that you can get a view of everyone in the room. Especially as female because we were constantly objectified by a bunch of horny inmates who would call you derogatory names because you ignore their sexual advances. I was everything but a child of God. You run the risk of being touched or groped. Then there are the rumors that start because you spend too much time talking to an inmate and don't get me wrong there were a few who decided to jeopardize their jobs by doing much more than just talking. In 2012 another female coworker and I took it upon ourselves to create a life skills program called G.I.F.T.S. by Empowering your Future which stands for Great Intelligence Further Transcend Success. We started the program because we wanted to make a difference in these young men lives. We presented the program to our Superintendent at the time who gave us the green light. Little did we know our program would be used against us. We found ourselves being investigated for "Socializing with an Offender". I was distraught because for the life of me I didn't understand how I could be accused of socializing with an offender when according to the mission statement it was our responsibility as staff to teach these young men how be social individuals. As our hearing went on and with supporting evidence, we were found to have done nothing wrong. This was a relief to us because we later found out that we were 30 days pending being fired. We would have had our character and good names damaged and working with children would have been out the question. This was the most stressful time in my career, and I turned to alcohol to suppress it. I found myself always stopping for dark rum or wine. I used it as way to numb how I felt about the job and to suppress the guilt that I felt. Remember in the beginning on my first day when I told myself that this wasn't what I wanted to do for the rest of my life. Easier said than done, right. Especially when your family and friends are on the outside looking in because to them it's a good paying job with benefits. Little did they know that you were drinking heavily, depressed and contemplating suicide. This the side of the job that no one talks about.

No one wants to talk about the health risk that come with the job; stress, high blood pressure, alcoholism, drug use, depression and suicide. Everyone sees it as your making good money why complain. So, I told myself I needed to make a change because being a CO is not all its cracked up to be. So, I decided I wanted to become a supervisor.

Supervisor

In 2015 I accepted the position as a supervisor with the department. This meant more money; I didn't have to work the unit and more importantly it looked good on my resume. Little did I know this would be just as bad if not worse. As everyone knows when it comes to a supervisory position you must deal with it all, paperwork, schedules, staff and higher ups. Now as a juvenile correctional supervisor you have one more extra job added to that, inmates. I thought that once I become a supervisor, I would deal with the inmates less. Unfortunately, that was not the case. I saw them now more than ever. Staff would always call when they had an uncooperative inmate who refused to follow a direct order. Inmates constantly wanting to talk to you about random things that were out of your control. Did I mentioned as female they wanted to be your face even more. As supervisor I also got mandated to work the overnight shift quite often because I was now at the bottom of the barrel for seniority. Let's not forget about dealing with upper management. They nit picking at everything that you do, the constant phone calls about frivolous things that were out of your control or things that they themselves could have addressed the moment it occurred. Your held at a higher standard once you become a supervisor. You are expected to step on the staff that helped you get to that position and trust me some supervisors had no issues doing it. I had on the other hand refused to do just that. I was told my a higher up to apologize to the superintendent because I ruffled his feather when I called him out in front of a group of staff. I told that higher up in these exact words, "I'm not apologizing for speaking the truth". He then stated, "you're a supervisor now and your held at a higher standard". I told him "what you fail to realize is that I don't give a damn about this black shirt, I will go back to being a blue shirt because this position is nothing but a resume filler for me". He looked appalled and I meant every word. The last thing I refused to do was let the color of my shirt or position that I'm in change who I am as person. In December of 2015 I found out I was pregnant. Once I notified my supervisor, I was placed on office duty. Of course, this didn't stop the multiple phone calls from staff dealing with uncooperative inmates. This time I was stuck talking to them on the phone to get them to comply. At one point I had to leave the office even though I wasn't supposed to because the inmate refused to lock up for the night and it was already approaching 9:30pm. On top of being pregnant and bound to the gate I was stuck doing all the paperwork for the shift. This became a problem further in my pregnancy because I developed carpal tunnel and it was the worst kind ever. No amount of therapy was going to help it. The doctor told me I simply had to have the baby. Once I had the baby, I was able to stay on maternity leave for about 3 months because being the person I am I saved up all the time I had. Let's just say it was the best 3 months of my life and I dreaded going back to that place. Upon returning to work after 3 months I was welcomed back with a new breed of inmates. Ones that climbed roofs and would stay there for hours on end. My first day back four inmates broke line movement after dinner and got on the roof of one the old buildings and refused to come down. It was around 9:30pm before they finally decided to come down. The rest of summer was spent talking inmates off the roof of buildings. So, when I got home, I made the decision to resign after November 9, 2016. Why I chose that date you ask, it was my 7-year anniversary date with the department. Plus, since I wasn't vested, I would be able to withdraw my pension which came at price and one that I was willing to take. On January 31, 2017 I walked out a free woman after doing a 7-year bid with the department. Now I know how the inmates felt on release day.

Chapter Two

Mother

First Time Mom

In December of 2015 I found out I was pregnant I wasn't immediately filled with joy. I cried and I was little bit angry with myself. This wasn't how I planned it. I wanted to be financial stable with two incomes in the household and married. In January I made an appointment with my Primary Care Physician. After doing the urine analysis I was informed that I was 3 months pregnant. Guilt immediately started to set in because I had been drinking quiet heavily before I found out I was pregnant. The stress of the job. My PCP then referred me to an OBGYN who schedule my ultrasound and various other appointments. My first and only ultrasound we found out we were having a boy. My boyfriend (now husband) wasn't surprised because he just knew it was a boy. A month went by and I went to see one of the OBGYN's on my team to check vitals and check the baby's heartbeat and boy did he have a strong heartbeat. I was informed that based on the gestation he would be due June 17, 2016 (Father's Day). I thought to myself perfect, I can kill two birds with one stone. A Father's Day gift for my dad and my boyfriend. As the month of March approached, I started developing carpal tunnel in both my hands. It felt as though someone was taking little pins and sticking them in my hand like a pin cushion. There were days when I couldn't feed or bath myself, so my boyfriend had to do it. The pain became so unbearable so I made an appointment with my PCP to see what I could do to relieve the pain. She said that there was nothing that could be done. I would simply have to give birth for it to go away. She told me I could also try physical therapy to help relieve some of the pressure. It worked for a little while. I decided that I would just have to suck it up and deal with it at this point since I only had a couple more months until the baby was born. On April 9th, 2016 I woke up with my hands and feet swollen so bad that they looked like a puffer fish. I didn't think much of it because this was my first pregnancy and I was told that your hands and feet would swell. As the day went on, I started getting a headache, so I decided to take a nap. I woke up few hours later and asked my boyfriend if he could get me some tacos. So, once he came back with them, I ate them and told him I was going back to bed because my head was still hurting. I was then awakened by a strange voice asking me a series of question, what's your name? when's your due date? As I'm being asked these questions, I could tell that I was in some sort of vehicle. I then felt a sharp prick in my arm and a gush of cold air as I passed out. When I woke, I saw my dad crying over me, along with my mom. I glanced around the room to see my brother, my cousin, my aunt, my boyfriend and his mother. I started to ask myself, "Am I dead, am I having an out a body experience?". I then see a nurse walk in and pull a tube out of my throat. I tried to talk but my voice was groggy. My boyfriend step towards me and began explaining to me that when he came to check on me, he found me seizing in the bed. He called 911 and they rushed me to the Emergency Room and when I got there I seized again. So, they had to preform an emergency c-section. Once they cut me open the baby had the umbilical cord around his neck. They had to air lift him to another hospital because the one I was at didn't have a NICU. The doctor came in and informed me that I had what was known as preeclampsia and that Ashton was believed at 29 weeks gestation. He informed me that it was a good thing that my boyfriend was at home because both me and the baby could have died. I spent the rest of week in the hospital not knowing what my son looked like. Then one day my boyfriend brought me a photo that the nurses at the NICU were nice enough to take of him. He looked so small and he had tubes attached to him. My heart started breaking because fear started rushing into my head that I could lose this little person that I didn't even get a chance to meet yet. That Friday I was released from the hospital and I was finally able to go see my son who was at another hospital that was a 45-minute drive from our home. When I walked into the NICU I could hear machines beeping and see little babies in incubators. My boyfriend guided me to the right which is where our baby was. As I walked closer the tag on his incubator read,

Name: Ashton

DOB: April 9, 2016

Time: 10:53pm

Weight: 2lbs 11oz

As looked at my son so small and helpless with a bunch of tubes coming out of him, I broke down crying. The nurse came in and asked if I wanted to hold him. I told her yes, when she handed him to me if he felt so light and he looked so tiny. They informed me that he's a strong baby and that he only stayed on the breathing machine for one night. As the weeks went on, I was there at the hospital everyday to see my son. I constantly checked his growth chart and asked as many questions as I could because from that day forward, I knew would have to be his advocate. Ashton showed progress and the tubes and IV's were removed with the acceptation of his feeding tube because he was still learning to suck, breath and swallow at the same time. In May 2016 I got the phone call that I had been waiting for. They informed me that Ashton could go home, I was overjoyed and excited to bring my baby home. As the month of June went on Ashton began to have some issues keeping his milk down and started breaking out in large sores. I also noticed a large bulge in his groin area. I immediately made an appointment with his pediatrician. She inspected the bulge and informed me that he had a hernia and referred me to a specialist. She had the nurse draw blood so that they could run some test to see why he was breaking out in large sores. Later in the week we were notified that Ashton had a milk allergy and that we would need to change his formula "Nutrimagen". During the midst of all this we were bouncing from specialist to specialist trying find someone that was willing to operate on a baby that small. We were finally able to find a doctor in our network that was willing to perform the hernia repair. The surgery was a success. As the rest of the year went on Ashton began to gain more weight and developed like a normally baby would. He did however develop the behavior of being picky with his food and would only eat fruits. He would gag when you put new food in front of him. The pediatrician stated that it was normal behavior for some babies to not want what you feed them. By the time Ashton turned one he was still picky about what he ate, he would only eat strawberries, grapes, oranges and mangoes. He refused to any meat products of any kind. He had also not started crawling or walking yet. He would just merely drag himself around the room. At around 15 months he started crawling, then he proceeded to stand and then walk all within one month. We were overjoyed. However, his speech had not developed yet, and his Pediatrician had concerns that he might be Autistic. They had someone come out the house and interview us about his behaviors. They informed us that it was too early to tell because he was so young. So, we left it alone. My family began to have concerns

and believed that Ashton had some hearing issues. We got his hearing

tested and he passed. So, at that point it became a waiting game.

However, the thought that my son might have a learning disability never

left my mind.

The Diagnosis

For those of us that have children, we know becoming a mother is one of the best feelings in the world. The question is what you do when you notice that your child is not developing like other children and doctors keep telling you to give it time. I personally refused to give it time. Ashton was 2 years old and still not talking and if he did say anything he would only say "da-da". So, as his advocate I requested that he be placed in Speech Therapy to see if that would help with his speech. I also informed his new pediatrician that I would like him tested for Autism and she agreed. She informed me that he should have hit his milestones and should be speaking by now. We were referred to a psychologist who we met with and she asked us a series of questions about his development, eating habits and anything we thought was out of the ordinary. We informed her that Ashton loved technology and caught on very quickly on how to use a tablet or a phone. He also had a very strange eating habit where he would only eat fruits and Cheerios. He still refused to eat meat. He had also developed an issue with texture and smell. He would turn his head away when you tried to introduce something new to him to eat. He also didn't play with toys the same way other kids would. Instead of sliding a car across the floor and stack blocks. He would simply spin the toy repeatedly in his hand or he would chew on them. On January 19, 2019 Ashton was scheduled to have the ADOS test. As I watched as the psychologist administer a series of test and observed Ashton's response, she would clearly see that he had no interest in doing anything. He began to get frustrated and had a meltdown in her office. She stated she got what she needed to determine the results and that she would have them to me by the following weekend. Along with the test I also had to answer a series of additional questions about his behaviors. On January 26, 2019 I met with the psychologist to go over the results of the test. As she turned each page, she explained what was written on them. When she turned to the final page, I could see the words "Diagnosis: Autistic". She began to explain to me to the diagnosis and she waited to see what my response was going to be. I informed her that I already knew that he was Autistic because I saw the signs. She informed me that I caught it early because not very many parents do. She informed me that the next step was to get him in Applied Behavioral Analysis Therapy for Autism (ABA). She also informed me that she recommends that he does 25 hours of ABA Therapy a week. She stated that this would be best thing to get him where he needs to be developmentally. I thanked her for assisting us in getting him tested and I left the office. Once I got in the car, I texted my husband and informed him of the results. He informed me that he wished he could be there for me in that moment and he asked me where we go from here. I informed him what the psychologist had told me. Later that week I had an appointment with his pediatrician who informed me that she would pass on the paperwork to Ashton's case manager who would put in the referral request for ABA Therapy. About a week later I was informed that he was approved and was given the name and phone number of the ABA center in town that I could go to. I contacted the center and scheduled an appointment with the centers Clinical Director. On February 25, 2019 we walked into the ABA center. As I walked in, I felt a sense of relief and good energy. I was greeted by a staff member and the Clinical Director. She informed me that she wanted to meet with me first and that Ashton could go to the back with the other kids. As I watched Ashton walk away, I found myself not having to explain to them how to deal with him and why he doesn't respond when they speak to him. As I sat in the office the clinical director read over his diagnosis and she began to ask me a series of questions. The main one that she asked was "what are your goals for Ashton?". I informed her that my goal for him was for him to be able to answer basic yes or no questions. I would also like to work on his issues with texture that we can get him to try new foods and of course potty training. She informed me that these were all great goals and ones that can be accomplished. She informed me she would write up his treatment plan and send it back to the insurance company and once she gets it back, he can begin his therapy sessions. I left the meeting with a sense of relief and a ton of weight lifted off my shoulders. Now I had someone who understood my son and knew what to do to help me. On March 6, 2019 Ashton started his first day at ABA Therapy. This would be the beginning of the journey to his success in life. When Ashton first started ABA Therapy it was rough in the beginning mainly because he hadn't been around anyone else except family. He would cry every day at drop off. As time went on, he got more comfortable with going to therapy and seeing the same faces, consistency is key with him. He started mastering a few of the goals that were set for him, but he had yet to say any real words. Eating table food was still an issue. So, I took him to see an allergist. She requested bloodwork and I was shocked when she gave me the results. He was only allergic to fish, more so Cod fish than anything. He no longer had a milk or citrus allergy; he was merely lactose intolerant which was something that runs on his dad side of the family. So, I decided to buy various food for him to try and still no success, he just won't try anything you put in front of him. I decided to try him with peanut butter and let's just say it was a bad idea. Within a few minutes he broke out in hives, his eyes became blood shot red and his eyes began to swell up. I immediately gave him some Benadryl and within 5-10 mins the allergic reaction began to subside. I immediately contacted his allergist and they informed me that he did test high for peanuts but because he tolerated it in the past, they assumed that it would be fine for him to consume it. I was appalled and I informed them that I need a physical copy of his allergy results. When I received the allergy results there were several things that were on the list that he tested high for. He tested high for corn, wheat, cod fish, sesame, peanut. So back to the drawing board I go of trying to find foods that he can consume that do not contain any of these items.

On August 19, 2019 Ashtons started his first day of Pre-K and I was excited for him. His dad took it a little hard because he was still on deployment for his sons first day of school. He didn't cry at drop off and neither did I. He had a good first day. As the weeks went on the teacher informed me that Ashton kind of does his own thing and doesn't really engage with the rest of class. I wasn't the least bit surprise. I informed the teacher that he would need a one on one aid that could keep him on task. In September the teacher sends me a message informing me that she thinks Ashton would be better suited in a classroom for children with Autism. I immediately advocated for my son. This is his first teacher and she was already giving up on him and was ready to pawn him off on someone else. I informed her that when I had a team meeting with Principal and other faculty members it was discussed, and I informed them I wanted him in a mainstream classroom with children that were not on the spectrum. I also reminded her that I requested that he had a one on one aid. I informed her that if he is not able to get an aid then I will be pulling him out of school and sending him to ABA Therapy only. She informed me that before I pulled him out of school, I would need to have a meeting with the team at the school. So, in October I had meeting with the team which included the principal. Each person gave me a brief on their interaction with my son. They also had the teacher who taught the classroom for children with Autism. She began explaining to me that she has two children in her classroom and that it can get a little hectic. As I'm watching her explain her classroom set up, she appeared a little frazzle. The last thing I want is a teacher who only has two children to be frazzled and attempting to teach my child. I still wasn't sold on the idea. The principal informed the team that they needed to come up with a better approach. I began explaining to them what he does at ABA Therapy and the teacher who teaches the ADS classroom began explaining to me that with ABA my son will lack social interaction. I informed her that my son gets plenty of social interaction with other children during playtime, snack time and lunch time. The principal then intervened and stated not to push the ASD classroom. The meeting ended and we decided to meet again and discuss his progress at parent teacher conferences. On October 22, 2019 we had parent teacher conference. At the conference was Ashton's teacher, the principal, the speech therapist for the school and another faculty member. The teacher proceeded to explain what they implemented to aid Ashton in his learning environment. She also informed us that he now has an aid. The principal stated that she feels he will thrive more if he stays in his current classroom. So, the meeting ended on a positive note and Ashton will be staying in the mainstream classroom. As I was leaving the school, I just kept thinking to myself, how many more teachers will I have to have this discussion with when they decide they don't want to work with my child because he's not speaking yet or because he doesn't interact like other children do. No matter how many, I'm ready for them all. On a more positive note he was doing amazing at ABA Therapy and they even hired a Speech Therapist. I love his team and they love working with him. Ashton began using PECS as a means of communication and it was working out great. His PECS communication binder had real photos of things he uses or requested daily. So, for example if he wanted cheerios, he would bring me the picture of cheerios. After winter break, we noticed a regression with the PECS, and he was using them more as a toy than a communication device. On February 21, 2020 Ashton had his IEP meeting. At the meeting they had propose yet again that Ashton be removed from the mainstream classroom and be put in a special program for children with Autism. I declined the program because my husband and I had already made the decision to remove him from school and focus more on therapy. A few weeks before his IEP meeting Ashton was falling asleep almost every day in school and at therapy they informed me he would immediately go to the kitchen after drop-off because he was hungry. It wasn't until a few days before his IEP meeting that his teacher informed me that he wasn't eating somedays during breakfast. They didn't take care to offer him his cheerios later. We were livid and it explained a lot of his behaviors. They had also not kept an open line of communication with his ABA therapist and had him doing things at school he had already mastered months earlier in therapy. For, example he had mastered tapping blocks together but in school they were trying to teach him to communicate the word "more" by tapping two dinosaurs together. I know you are all thinking "that doesn't make sense", my thoughts exactly. Since his removal from school he has been in a better mood and is more focused at ABA.

Third Pregnancy, Second Child

My husband and I decided that we wanted to have more children. On September 28, 2018 we found out we were pregnant. We were overjoyed, and he began picking out names because he knew it was another boy. We called our family and friends and told them the good news. Some were excited for us and some asked me if that was the best move since my husband was getting deployed in a few months. That struck a nerve because here I am 33 years old and people are asking me if that was a good decision. I just didn't understand why they couldn't just say congratulations and leave it at that. On September 30, 2018 I told my husband something didn't feel right after having intercourse. So, I went to the bathroom and realized I was spotting a little. My husband instantly went into panic mode. I told him to calm down and we will keep watching to see if gets worse. As the day went on the bleeding became heavier. I informed my husband that I think I might be having a miscarriage. I could see the devastation in his eyes. I informed my husband that I would call the doctors office Monday to see if they had any open appointments. On Monday October 1, 2018 at 9am I was able to get in and see my PCP. She had me go to the lab to get blood work complete and to radiology to get a vaginal ultrasound completed. At the end of the day I received a phone call from my PCP, and she informed me that I was pregnant and that my body was spontaneously aborting the fetus and according to the bloodwork I was about two weeks pregnant. I went home and I informed my husband what the doctor said, he was devasted. As the week went on, he informed me that he made an appointment for us to meet with the Chaplin so we could do grieve counseling and he also signed us for a couple's retreat. We listened to the Chaplin and his wife talk about how they dealt with their miscarriage. As we were talking their youngest son who was about 2 years old came and sat in his mom's lap. They then informed us that he was their rainbow baby. They conceived him right after the miscarriage. After leaving the meeting my husband and I held hands and we knew we were going to be ok and that we could always try again. On November 1, 2018 my husband and I along with son went to Kansas City, Missouri for the "Strong Bonds" retreat which was sponsored by the military for couples. On Friday November 2, 2018 I decided to take another pregnancy test and low and behold it was positive. My husband was super excited and so was I. We decided to not tell our family until we got further along in the pregnancy. Later in the month we went in for a doctor's appointment and had blood work completed. The doctor also scheduled an ultrasound. The ultrasound revealed that I had 3 fibroids. The rest of year was filled appointments to monitor the pregnancy and fibroids. In January of 2019 we found out that we were having a girl and that our due date was July 11, 2019. My husband was not too excited about it because he wanted another boy. As time went on it grew on him and he picked out her name just like he did our son. He decided he wanted to name her "Amelia". I for one didn't like the name at first but it grew on me plus it's the least I could do since I'm getting a girl. I will admit that this pregnancy was rough on me because I was doing it by myself since my husband ended up deploying at the end of January 2019. As time went on and I got into a routine and things got easier. Going to appointments alone and having doctors overwhelm me with information. The doctor informed me that they wanted to do a scheduled

C-Section on July 4, 2019 which I agreed. As time went on, I started developing carpal tunnel again like I did with Ashton around 28th or 29th week of my pregnancy. Around 34-35 weeks is when it began to get worse. It started off with just a tingle sensation in my right hand. Then it went to my two middle fingers going numb on my right hand and the numbness spreading to the palm of hand. There were nights when I would wake up in so much pain, I had to sit on the edge of the bed dangling my arms to the side to get any kind of relief. At my next doctor's appointment, I mentioned it to the doctor, and she said that there wasn't anything she could do, the only thing that would rid me of the pain is having the baby. At this appointment she overwhelmed me with even more information on what to expect on the day of delivery, let's just say I was terrified. As you recall I was unconscious for Ashtons birth because of preeclampsia. This time I would be awake and made aware of everything that was happen. She informed me that the day before the C-Section that I would need to go to the lab to get blood work so that they can know my blood type. They needed the information to ensure that they had enough blood on standby just in case I hemorrhaged and needed a blood transfusion. I was so terrified after that and I wanted to cry because I just had a family member that went through that. On July 1st my husband was scheduled to arrive home for 10 days for the birth of the baby. I had to drive 2 hours to Kansas City International airport to pick him up with Ashton in toe. On July 3, 2019 at 1am I started having contractions, so my husband took me to the hospital. When we arrived at labor and deliver, they took me to a room and hooked me up to a machine to monitor the baby and my contractions. They informed me that they were only 5-7 minutes apart and I was only about ½ centimeter dilated. It took them 3 times to find a vein to administer an IV which was painful. I spent the next 4 hours laying in the hospital bed and was still only ½ centimeters dilated. So, they decided to send me home. They informed me that if they get closer then come back. On July 4, 2019 at 1am my contractions became stronger and they were 2-3 minutes apart. My husband again took me to the hospital. Once I got to labor and deliver, they took me straight to maternity ward and hooked me up to a machine to monitor my contractions. They checked my cervix and I was already 4 centimeters dilated. Since I had a scheduled C-section there was no need to wait for me to be dilated even more. They began looking for a vein to administer the IV and again it took them 3 tries' before finding a vein. I was in so much pain between the needle pokes and the contractions. They informed me and my husband that because it was before visiting hours kids were not allowed in the room or the OR so our son couldn't stay. So, my husband had to leave and take our son home and I was left at the hospital by myself. The nurse proceeded to walk me to the OR and once I walked in, I felt like I had walked into an icebox. It was so cold, sterile and bright. They had me sit on the bed and the Anesthesiologist proceeds to administer a numbing agent to numb my skin. As I sat there squeezing the nurse's hand I began to cry because yet again I was all alone delivering my baby and unlike the first time I was awake and aware of what was happening. As the Anesthesiologist began to administer the epidural, I could feel something courses through my body on the left side. I began to scream, and the Anesthesiologist asked what side of my body I was feeling pain and I screamed "THE LEFT". Its hard to describe what it felt like but let's just say it felt like someone was pumping hot fluid into my veins. As I sat there a million thoughts were going through my head. I needed my husband because he was my support system and we were supposed to do this together. The Anesthesiologist stopped what she was doing and asked me if I wanted to just do general anesthesia and I replied "yes". So, they proceeded to administer general anesthesia and I went to sleep. When I woke up, I was being moved from the OR back to my room. When I got in the room, I saw our baby girl. Her name tag read:

"Name: Amelia

Date: July 4, 2019

Time: 4:04am

Weight: 5lbs 14oz

I laid in the bed and I began to cry again because it wasn't 6am yet and my husband and son were not there yet. When 6am rolled around I got excited because they walked right in my room. As laid in the bed in pain the nurse informed me that they had me on a morphine drip. As the day went on, I requested to be taken off the drip because it was making me dizzy and nauseous. I also had thrown up several times that day. Every

few hours the nurse would apply pressure to my stomach and check my

incision. On July 5th the doctor came to see me and informed me that I

could go home on Saturday July 6th. On July 6th, 2019 we were released

from the hospital. Being at home was an easy adjustment. I was still in

pain and I had to sleep on the couch because laying flat in our bed was

uncomfortable. On July 8th, 2019 my parents arrived to help us with the

Amelia and Ashton. On July 11, 2019 my husband had to return to

Germany. The entire drive to Kansas City International Airport I had a

million thoughts going through my head. After dropping him off at the

airport I began to cry and started thinking about the experience that I had

while delivering our baby girl and the fact that my husband had to head

back overseas and how much I was going to miss him. Having my

parents visit was a huge help because I was able to rest, and my mom

cooked almost every day. On July 17, 2019 I had my first post op

appointment and the doctor removed the glue from my incision and

informed me that my incision had healed nicely. On July 18, 2019 my

parents returned home and not having them here to help was hard the first night. As the days went on, I got into a routine with both kids. There were days when I was so exhausted that I couldn't see straight and would cry. I missed having the help, but I wouldn't trade them for anything in the world. In August my mother in law came to visit for a week which was very helpful. I was able to get a break and even went to dinner with few of the ladies I met at the military base.

Chapter Three

Wife

The Breadwinner

I've been working since the age of 16 and didn't stop working up until August 2018. As an individual I liked working and making money to support myself. Once I was in a serious relationship that thought went out the window once I became the breadwinner. It's the most stressful job known to man. Having to be the one responsible for your household and paying all the bills is no easy task. It can cause fights and friction in your relationships. I believe it stemmed from my dad instilling in me that I must be able to take care of myself so that I don't have to depend on anyone else to do it. So, I ran with it. Over the years in my relationships I found myself dating men that either made less money than me or didn't work at all. I always told myself that they would need me more than I ever needed them. So, when I started dating my boyfriend who later became my husband, I never set any expectations for him. I never informed him that I need him to have a job or contribute to the household because he was in school at the time. As the years went on, he became more comfortable with not working and I became more stressed. We would always get into arguments about finances which is the number reason why most relationships fail. When I tried to encourage him to get a job it would turn into a huge argument and I for one don't like conflict in my house because it wasn't something that I was used to growing up as kid. Once our son was born, it became easier for me to accept him not working because he now fell into the roll of stay at home dad. I was ok with it because we were saving on childcare and with Ashton being born 29 weeks premature, I just didn't trust anyone around him. I finally reached my breaking point when we moved to Arizona and the job market wasn't as lucrative as back in Illinois. I was making $40,000 less than what I made back home in a position I was overqualified for. Not to mention I had started going back to school. I found myself physically drained and emotionally exhausted. Some days I found myself screaming at the top of my lungs and pulling my hair on the ride home from work. Then the arguments started between my husband and I because there were days when I would come home late from work. One day I was coming home from work late and we got into a heated argument over the phone and I was screaming at top of my lungs. I contemplated veering off the road and killing myself, but I quickly remembered that I had a child that loved me and was depending on me. When I got home that night, I barely spoke to my husband. I instead went and took a shower and started crying. I prayed and I prayed to God for an answer on what I should do next. I also failed to mention that we had fell behind on our car payment, rent and bills. So, the next day I quit my job without telling my husband. I got a phone call from the company who I had my car loan through who informed me that they were in the process of repossessing my car. We were also about to be evicted from our apartment. So, I called my mom that day crying and her exact words to me was "COME HOME". That was my answer from God. So, we sold everything that we owned and packed whatever we could into the SUV and made that 21-hour drive back to Illinois. I'm a sure a lot of people will be shocked when they read this and will be in complete disbelief. Some are going to blame my husband but, I am to be blamed as well because like I stated before I never stated my expectations. I personally liked the idea of being the breadwinner because it gave me a sense of power. A power that became to much and almost drove me to committing suicide. So, the day I relinquished the crown was bittersweet. I was excited to not be the breadwinner, but I didn't like the fact that I was not working. Stay at home mom was a title that I would have to settle into.

Being a Military Spouse

When my husband and I decided he would join the military, it was a tough decision for us because that meant leaving his family especially our son. On April 9, 2018 my husband left for bootcamp. It was a hard day for me because it was also our son's birthday as well. I kept a brave face for my husband but once I got in the car I started crying. This would begin my journey as a military spouse and our life as a military family. The two months was spent waiting on letters in the mail since that was their only source of communication. Getting a letter in the mail from my husband was the highlight of my day. As I read some of the letters, I has happy and sad. There were lots of apologies and regrets of what we could have done better to make our lives easier. We also uplifted each other and made promises to see this through. The military saved our marriage. My husband went through a tough time in the during bootcamp because I wasn't there for him to lean on, so he depended on my letters as words of encouragement to get him through those tough times. On June 19, 2018 Ashton and I set out to Fort

Jackson military base in South Caroline to see his dad after two months of not physically seeing him. On June 20, 2018 we were sitting in the bleachers for family day when the commander informed us that we could go down to the field and find our solider. I went down to the field with our son Ashton on my hips within search of his father. It took me a while to find him because he was not the person we remembered. When he left us, he had a full head of hair and a full beard and built. When I finally found him, he reminded me of a younger version of himself from high school. He looked a lot younger, bald head, no facial hair and had lost a weight. He was so excited to see us that he couldn't stop hugging us. We went back to the hotel on base. We picked up were left off as a family. We watched Netflix and he ate a Charley's philly cheese steak sandwich as he first real meal in two months. The next day June 21, 2018 my husband graduated from boot camp. His mother was able to make it to graduation and just like me she didn't recognize him at first. That day we spent the day hanging out. Later that afternoon we had to drop him back off at the barracks and say goodbye. On June 22, 2018 my husband left Fort Jackson to make his way to AIT (Advance

Individual Training) at Fort Lee military base in Virginia. While at Fort Lee things were a little bit easier on us because he had access to his phone, and he was able to call and FaceTime us. He would spend the next two months training for his MOS (Military Occupational Specialty). On August 22, 2018 my husband graduated from AIT and immediately hop on a plane to come home. I drove to St. Louis International Airport to pick him up and looked the same as a remembered him on Family Day at boot camp except he had hair on his head. We begin that drive back to Springfield, IL and talked about everything under the sun. The next day August 23, 2018 we set out to drive 6 hours to Fort Riley military base in Kansas with Ashton and our family pet Bella in toe to embark on our new journey as military family. Upon arriving at the military base, we had to spend eight days living out of our luggage in a hotel until our housing on the military base was ready. On August 31, 2018 we moved into our home on Fort Riley military base. We moved into a nice 3-bedroom 2 bath home which was plenty of space for the three of us. We slowly adjusted to the military lifestyle. My husband worked a weird schedule, so I spent most of my day hanging out with our son.

As time went on, we settled into our routine as a military family until my husband informed me that he was being deployed for 9 months. I knew that at some point this would happen, and I mentally prepared myself a little. He informed me that he would be leaving January 2019. When January rolled around, and it was time for my husband to leave it was very hard. I had come to realization that it would be just me and Ashton on top of that I was about 3 months pregnant. The day he left I had to drop him off at this company, I managed to hold it together until I got back home and that's when the tears came. I would be spending the next 9 months as single parent to our son while being pregnant. As the months went one it got a little easier because I was able keep busy with school and taking Ashton to his therapy sessions. I will say this, being a military spouse is no walk in the park. It's a title that comes with laughter, joy, pain, anger, frustration and resentment. Then there are roles that you take on such as secretary, financial consultant, therapist and spiritual advisor. It became a little overwhelming at times especially being pregnant. There were lots of arguments about finances and each person's spending habits. I'm not going to lie I resented my husband a little because I felt as though every other weekend, he was out having fun while I was sitting at home taking care of our son while also carrying our daughter. He would always FaceTime or text me to let me know where he was going and letting me know that he wishes I was there with him. I can honestly say there were times when I didn't want to know because knowing would only upset me even more. Then looking at our bank account and see the amount of transactions he would make in one weekend would just send me over the edge. I did my best to monitor and watch is spending habits which would also cause more arguments when I pointed it out to him, he would get upset. Money is one of my biggest stressors and I was beyond stress. I had to keep reminding myself that I had to stay in the right frame of mind for our daughter.

One thing they fail to mention is that when your spouse is deployed your going to be managing two households. We only had once source of income and spending money for two households. While my husband was deployed, I had to send him care packages with toiletries, snacks and any thing that they may need. As I watch our accounts dwindle, I began to have regrets about getting pregnant before he deployed. I kept thinking to myself that I could be working and bringing in a second income. It also didn't help that he would drop sudden hints about you being a stay at home parent and how easy I had it. I began to have regrets on wanting to stay at home, it was supposed to be an enjoyable moment, but I wasn't really enjoying it because it would lead to us arguing about money. Once he got back from deployment got better and we got on the same page when it came to finances.

Student

In 2017 my husband convinced me to go back to school and get my master's degree. I wasn't sure what to get my degree in. I hadn't been back to school since I graduated with my bachelors in 2008. He suggested something in the medical field which I was against because I had no interest in working in the medical field. It wasn't an interest when the suggestion was made to me back in 2004 by a family member when I started my undergrad and it will never be an interest of mine. After a couple of weeks, I finally decided on a major. I chose to get my master's in Public Administration. I chose this major because I had an interest in learning how policies and procedures worked within the government and maybe someday get an opportunity to put my stamp in government and be a part of writing a policy. In October 2017 I started my MPA program with University of Phoenix. I chose to complete my program online because it worked best with my schedule and gave a lot of flexibility. It was a struggle at first balancing being a mom, wife, student and having a career. I continued to focus on the fact that I was doing this for my son and later my daughter. In June 2019 I completed my MPA Program and in October 2019 I began my Human Resource Management Certificate Program. I decided to pursue the HRM program because I wanted to keep my options open career wise. I schedule to complete the program March 2020. I need to set an example for my children and going back to school was one of them.

Chapter Four

Christian

Faith

I have always been involved in the church ever since I was little, from Sunday school, youth choir, vacation Bible school, etc. If it was church related, I was involved. I was taught at a very young age to always call on God when I needed him no matter the circumstances. I came from a family of prayer warriors who were also heavily involved in the church. I remember having to recite Bible verses and having to write essays about them. As I got older, I decided that I didn't need to physically be in a church to still have a connection to God. It is because of my connection to God and my faith in him is the one of the main reasons as to why I never acted on my suicidal thoughts. Each time the thought crossed my mind I would scream out to God and ask why me and low and behold I would get an answer as to why me. God is my foundation and my rock. My husband always said that the universe always had a way of working things out in my favor and I believe him. My faith has kept me going all these years and like the saying goes "what doesn't kill me makes me stronger" has always been true for me.

In each and everyone of these stages in my life I always called on God and prayed that he sees me through it and once I came through victorious, I thanked him for it. This book was one of the hardest decisions I have ever had to make in my life because this meant exposing myself to family, friends and coworkers to a side of me that no one knew about. Letting people know that I suffered from depression and contemplated committing suicide was hard but like Elder and my dear friend told me someone needs to hear your story. So, I say this to you if your going through something hold on to your faith whatever it may and pray to your god, he or she will bring you through. Share your story because you just never know who might be going through what your going through.

Closing

The wrote this book within hopes that it reaches someone and lets them know that they are not alone. There are lots of people in the world that battle depression and contemplate committing suicide. Just hold on to your faith or your god and if you don't have any reach out to someone. Friends and family pay attention to the signs and reach out. When you feel overwhelmed find an outlet, something to help you destress and regroup.

"Cause chances are never given they token like interceptions"
~Meek Mill

88652768R00038